On Frequent Journeys

Worship Resources on Uprooted Peoples

Edited by Rebekah Chevalier

UNITED CHURCH PUBLISHING HOUSE
Toronto, Ontario

On Frequent Journeys
Worship Resources on Uprooted Peoples

Copyright © 1997 United Church Publishing House

All biblical qutations, unless otherwise noted, are from the *New Revised Standard Version Bible*, copyright © 1989, by the Division of Christian Education of the National Council of the Churches of Christ in the United States of America. Used by permission.

Care has been taken to trace ownership of copyright material contained in this text. The publisher will gratefully accept any information that will enable it to rectify any reference or credit in subsequent printings.

Canadian Cataloguing in Publication Data

Main entry under title:

On frequent journeys : worship resources on uprooted peoples

Includes bibliographical references.
ISBN 1-55134-074-7

1. Refugees - Prayer-books and devotions. I Chevalier, Rebekah, 1960- .

BV4596.R405 1997   242'.4'08691   C97-931246-9

United Church Publishing House
3250 Bloor Street West, Fourth Floor
Etobicoke, Ontario
Canada M8X 2Y4
416-231-5931
bookpub@uccan.org

Design and production: Department of Publishing and Graphics
Editor: Ruth Chernia
Cover photo of Mozambican child by Peter Williams/World Council of Churches.

Printed in Canada
5 4 3   03 02 01 00 99 98

 970112

Contents

An Invitation __

Today, we are witnessing in our world a movement of people unprecedented in its scale. There are between 100 million and 120 million migrants, refugees, and displaced people in the world — that's more than 1 in 50! No country is unaffected by the phenomenon of uprooted people.

The urgency of this global situation led the World Council of Churches' Central Committee to adopt unanimously a statement on uprooted people on September 22, 1995. The statement challenges churches worldwide to address uprooted people as a major crisis of our time, and to take bold actions to become the church of the stranger by welcoming and standing with refugees, migrants and other displaced people. (There are excerpts from the statement on page 9.)

The World Council of Churches also has issued an invitation to churches around the world to mark an Ecumenical Year of Churches in Solidarity with the Uprooted, defining "uprooted people" as all those forced to leave their homelands for political, environmental, and economic causes.

Why This Book?

As Christian communities, one of the fundamental ways we come together to express our faith is through worship. Our times of worship thus become important opportunities to remember those who are uprooted, and to commit ourselves to working for justice on their behalf. The wealth of worship material in this book will make it easier for those planning and leading worship to lift up this important theme.

How To Use This Book

The material may be used by people planning worship services, as well as those looking for devotional material to use during a meeting or gathering. Readers may choose one of the complete worship service outlines found in this book or may pick and choose from the material to create their own service. Whatever way you use this material, it is important to keep the following in mind:

- choose material that will work best in your setting, and adapt or supplement it as needed to suit your context;
- if possible, try to refer in some way to uprooted people in your own community or country. This may be as simple as adding several lines to a prayer lifting up uprooted people in your region; or may mean seeking out uprooted people to take part in your worship, always remembering the need for sensitivity, since some may not feel able to share their stories.

Rebekah Chevalier, May 1997

A Moment to Choose
Risking to be with Uprooted People

O n every continent, people are being torn from their homes by violence and despair. Millions of people have been displaced and wait for a chance to go home. As wars drag on, economies deteriorate and environments become more fragile, solutions for the uprooted are becoming more elusive. Governments in every region are closing their borders. Too many churches are also turning away from the strangers arriving on their doorsteps.

Behind the massive global dimensions of today's uprooting are individual stories of pain, of families being torn apart, of despair and suffering. More than one in every fifty human beings is now a refugee or international migrant. Most are women, youth, and children. The vast majority leave countries in the South and remain in the South.

People leave their communities for many reasons and are called by different names — refugees, internally displaced, asylum-seekers, economic migrants. As churches, we lift up all those who are *compelled* by severe political, economic and social conditions to leave their land and their culture — regardless of the labels they are given by others. Uprooted people are those forced to leave their communities: those who flee because of persecution and war, those who are forcibly displaced because of environmental devastation and those who are compelled to seek sustenance in a city or abroad because they cannot survive at home.

Although it has accelerated in recent years, the movement of people has been a permanent feature of human history. The reality is that we all live in multi-cultural, multi-ethnic, multi-religious, multi-lingual societies — though sometimes we don't *see* the strangers as Christ among us. When churches close themselves to the

From a "Statement on Uprooted People" adopted by the Central Committee of the World Council of Churches, September 22, 1995.

strangers in their midst, when they no longer strive for an inclusive community as a sign and foretaste of the Kingdom to come, they lose their reason to be.

We challenge the churches worldwide to rediscover their identity, their integrity and their vocation as the church of the stranger. Service to uprooted people has always been recognized as diaconia — although it has been peripheral to the life of many churches. But we affirm that it is also an ecclesial matter. As stated in Matthew 25:31–46, we are a church of the stranger — the church of Jesus Christ the stranger.

As government policies become more restrictive and public hostility against foreigners intensifies in every region, churches are challenged as never before to make a choice: will they choose to be the church of the stranger and take the side of the uprooted or will they choose to turn away or ignore the problem? Will they just refer questions about uprooted to their program for refugees or will they be the expression of the universality of the gospel and home to those who seek to claim their human dignity?

In some countries, to work with the uprooted is dangerous. In many places, to respond to the uprooted is not popular with local congregations who are concerned with the many pressing problems "among our own people." When we challenge the causes of injustice that uproot people, the church must be prepared to pay the price of confronting established powers and privilege.

This statement is directed to churches. As a Christian household, we must acknowledge and confess our failings. And we must move on to conversion and renewal. The credibility of our witness and advocacy must be based on our experience and engagement as well as on our convictions.

Prayers & Litanies

Affirmation of Faith

Leader: In response to the word, let us stand and affirm our
          faith:

All: We are all held in the hollow of God's hand,
          loved children of the universe,
          born from the life which flows from God,
          freed to the fullness of God's creation
          with all its beauty and variety.

          We are all worth dying for in Christ Jesus,
          all called to risen life in Christ's rising.
          The way of Jesus gives us footprints for our following
          and all our trials and longings are known
          in the frailty of Christ's birth among us
          and the courage of Christ's walking with us.

          We are all called to new things in the Spirit,
          in the hope that stirs in unlikely moments,
          the home we find in the wastelands of our wanderings,
          the warmth that we touch in the coldness of our need
          and the opening of our hearts to adventures in belonging
          or the gathering in of those without a home.

From the *Liturgy for Human Rights Sunday* prepared by the Christian Conference of Asia and
the Uniting Church in Australia, October, 1996.

At Prayer

with Children on the Street

S treet children have become part of the global urban landscape. As many as 100 million children live and work on the streets; a quarter of them have no other home. Forty percent live in Latin America. Hostages of global economics, they are threatened daily — as in the example of Daniel — by hunger, violence, drugs, and disease.

> A voice was heard in Ramah,
> wailing and loud lamentation,
> Rachel weeping for her children;
> She refused to be consoled
> because they are no more.
>
> — Jeremiah 31:15 —

Prayer

Mothering God,
open me to the pleading of this lamentation
    from Sao Paulo.
Open me — imagination, heart, and prayer —
    to the children of our world.
Help me in today's quiet to enter Daniel's pain
    and to join him in his hope:

Daniel, author of "Daniel's Song," is part of the Community Alternatives Project, founded and directed by Rev. Zeni de Lima Soares, the first woman Methodist pastor in Brazil. Used with permission. Text from *For the Healing of the Nations*, Church World Service Office on Global Education (OGE), 2115 N. Charles Street, Baltimore, MD 21218-5755; phone 410-727-6106; fax 410-727-6108.

Daniel's Song

If this street, if this street were mine
I would order Mrs. Hunger to go for a walk
And put on each post an inscription:
It is forbidden for a child not to have bread!

If this street, if this street were mine
I would order the exploiter to another place, and
On each corner only one voice would be heard:
Violence no longer lives among us!

If this street, if this street were mine
I would tear down the Forest of Loneliness
And shout in the new meadow:

Children are safe here!

Prayer

God of Daniel, let us meet him in the meadow,
life-filled and welcoming.
I unite my learnings and activities this day with Daniel's struggle.
We ask your Presence.
We trust its hovering.
We know its promise in Jesus Christ.
Amen.

_____ The Prayers of the People __

The symbols are brought forward during the prayers, or they may be placed on a small table covered with a cloth and brought forward at the Preparation of the Gifts if there is a celebration of the eucharist. Or they may remain on the table throughout the service. The symbols used may be indicated in the service leaflet.

Intercessions

Let us pray:

Silence is kept.

We remember before God all those who have been uprooted
    from their homes and communities;
    people who are compelled to flee for their lives,
    to leave their land and culture,
    and live apart from their families.

With them, we mourn their loss of dignity, community,
    resources, and employment.

A globe, map, or small bag with a few items of clothing may be brought forward as symbols of those who are uprooted.

We especially pray for the women
    who are the majority of those displaced.

We remember the work that women do
    to keep families together,
    to nurture community
    and end violence and injustice.

A shawl or a scarf may be brought forward.

Primate's World Relief and Development Fund, Anglican Church of Canada

We remember the millions of children
  whose lives are marked by danger and exploitation.

A worn child's shoe, or a small toy may be brought forward.

We remember those who are persecuted
  because of their gender, race, or creed.

We pray for the women and the men,
  the children, and the elderly,
  who seek safety and solace,
  who yearn to begin new lives.

For all the uprooted,

> **Sheltering God, in your mercy,**
> **Hear our prayer.**

We remember before God
  those countries where people must leave their homes
  because of war, injustice, and violence.

A figure of a dove, a paper crane, or a flower may be brought forward as symbols of peace.

We remember those places
  which have been made unsafe by land mines,
  and all those who have been killed or maimed by land mines.

We remember those in our own homeland
  who live with violence and its brutal threat.

For all people terrified by violence,

> **Gentle God, in your mercy,**
> **Hear our prayer.**

We pray for those who leave their homes for economic survival;
  we remember that the gap between rich and poor gets wider,
  and the earth's resources are shared by fewer people.

Pennies, newspaper clippings, or a food bank bag may be brought forward as symbols of economic survival.

We pray for those who pay the cost of international debt
    with their lives.

We remember the homeless and poorly housed
    and the unemployed in our own communities.

For all people displaced by economic disparity,

> **God of justice, in your mercy,**
> **Hear our prayer.**

We remember before God
    those who leave their homes because of earthquakes,
    storms, floods, and other disasters.

We acknowledge the effects of deforestation,
    degradation of farm land,
    nuclear and weapons testing,
    and the exploitation of resources
    for the sake of consumers in other countries.

A pot of earth, or an unpotted plant may be brought forward as symbols of the environment.

We remember those in our own communities
    who have been hurt by poor stewardship of creation.

For all people displaced by devastation of your world,

> **Creator God, in your mercy,**
> **Hear our prayer.**

We give thanks to you, God,
    for the world's diversity of peoples and cultures.

A multicoloured braid of wool, kaleidoscope, or rainbow may be brought forward as symbols of diversity.

We pray that hostility and indifference
    may give way to hospitality and justice
    in Canada and throughout the world.

Help us to be vigilant stewards and faithful partners,
    and strengthen us to live as people of your creation,
    committed and bold in deeds of justice.

God of all,
>   you taught us through your Son
>   to seek the signs of your reign
>   in the tiny mustard seed.
Plant your word deep in the soil of our hearts,
>   sow in us the seeds of compassion;
>   let your hospitality take root within us,
>   and your compassion grow in us,
>   so righteousness may spring forth in all the world,
>   and your holy will be done.
We ask this in his name.
Amen.

At this time, members of the congregation are invited to come forward and plant a seed as a sign of hope, and to name the hope aloud, concluding with the words "Come Holy Spirit."

Response:

> ***Renew the face of the earth
> and the hearts of your people.***

The Peace

The peace of the Lord be always with you.

> ***And also with you.***

_____ **Prayer of Commitment** __

Sisters and brothers,
 let us stand and affirm what we have discovered
 of God's will in the company of each other.

That we worship one God,
 Father, Son and Holy Spirit,
 in whose image we are made,
 to whose service we are summoned,
 by whose presence we are renewed,

This we believe.

That it is central to the mission of Christ
 to participate, by word and action,
 in the struggles of the poor for justice,
 to share justly the earth's land and resources,
 to rejoice in the diversity of human culture,
 to preserve human life in all its beauty and frailty,
 to accompany the uprooted and to welcome the stranger,
 and to witness — every day — to the love of God
  for people of the earth,

This we believe.

That we are called to become the Church of the Stranger,
 to open ourselves
 to the transforming power of the Holy Spirit
 which may come to us through the foreigner,
 to take the risk of speaking out
  on behalf of those who are different from us,

From the worship book used at the consultation The Prophetic Mission of Churches in Response to Forced Displacement of People held in Addis Ababa, Ethiopia, November 1995, co-sponsored by Caritas Internationalis, Lutheran World Federation/World Service, and the World Council of Churches.

and to see that when we minister to the stranger,
the uprooted,
we are serving our Lord and Saviour.

This we believe.

That God has called the church into being
to be the servant of the kingdom,
to be a sign of God's new order,
to celebrate in the streets and fields of every land
the liturgy of heaven,

This we believe.

That Christ, fully aware of our differences,
prays that we might be one
so that the world may believe

This we believe
and to this we are committed
for the love of God,
in the way of Christ,
by the power of the Holy Spirit. Amen.

How Strong I Am!

I never realised how strong I am as a woman. I always thought I was dependent on my family ... In [asylum country] I realised that I couldn't depend on people all the time ... I was only a teenager then ... I have faced life and death problems ... I was forced to think beyond my age ... sometimes you think there is no way out ... you have to struggle to survive as a refugee ...

From *A Moment to Choose: Risking to be with Uprooted Peoples*, A Resource Book produced by the World Council of Churches, 1996.

Iran. Afghan refugees, Sabzevar reception and quarantine camp.

UNHCR / 16049 / 11.1987 / A. Hollmann

Candleholder:
> Listen, I stand at the door and knock.
> If anyone hears my voice and opens the door,
> I will come into the house.
> I will eat with those who live there,
> and they shall eat with me.

Leader: Come, Lord Jesus, be our guest; stay with us,
for the day is ending.
Bring to our house your poverty.

All: *For then shall we be rich.*

Leader: Bring to our house your pain.

All: *That, sharing it, we may also share your joy.*

Leader: Bring to our house your understanding of us.

All: *That we may be freed to learn more of you.*

Leader: Bring to our house all those who hurry or hirple*
behind you.

All: *That we may meet you as the saviour of all.*

Leader: With friend, with stranger,
With neighbour and the well-known ones,
Be among us this night.

All: *For the door of our house we open, and the doors of our hearts we leave ajar.*

* Limp.

From *The Iona Community Worship Book* (Wild Goose Publications, 1988) by John L. Bell copyright ©1988 Wild Goose Resource Group, Iona Community, 188 Govan Road, Glasgow G51 3UU Scotland.

___ Prayer of Silent Confession ___

Silent confession (all kneeling)

Leader: Let us pray.

O God, our Father, we confess with shame our slowness to learn from Jesus Christ, the way, the truth and the life; and our reluctance to follow him. Thou hast met us in our neighbour and we have passed by; we have taken great benefits with little thanks; we have been unworthy of the changeless love.

Have mercy upon us and forgive us O Lord.

Forgive us when our worship is poor, the formality and selfishness of our prayers, our inconstancy and unbelief, our hypocrisy and our wilful ignorance of thy ways.

Have mercy upon us and forgive us, O Lord.

Forgive us where we have wasted our time or misused our gifts. Forgive us where we have evaded our responsibilities. Forgive us that we have been unwilling to overcome evil with good, that we have shrunk from bearing the cross.

Have mercy upon us and forgive us, O Lord.

If we have made no ventures in fellowship; if we have kept in our heart a grievance against another; if we have not sought reconciliation; if we have been eager for the punishment of wrong-doers; and slow to seek redemption.

Have mercy upon us and forgive us, O Lord, Amen.

Prepared by the Committee for the Week of Prayer and Confession in Africa, which was marked June 16–23, 1996.

Forgive us for turning our backs to the uprooted, and causing them to suffer.

Forgive us that we have denied them good food, shelter and love. We have paid deaf ears to their heartfelt needs and refused to share what we have with them.

Forgive us where we have rejoiced in their suffering.

Help us O Lord to welcome them into our homes; defend their cause, and be in solidarity with them in their daily struggles in life.

Have mercy upon us and forgive us, O Lord. Amen.

The Covenant

(All kneeling)

Leader: O Lord God, Holy Father,
who has called us through Christ
to be partakers in this gracious covenant,
we take upon ourselves with joy the yoke of obedience,
and engage ourselves for love of thee,
to seek and do thy perfect will.
We are no longer our own but thine.

All: I am no longer my own but thine;
put me to what thou wilt; rank me with whom thy wilt;
put me to doing, put me to suffering;
let me be employed for thee or laid aside for thee:
exalted for thee or brought low for thee;
let me be full, let me be empty, let me have all things;
let me have nothing;
I freely and heartily yield all things
    to thy pleasure and disposal.
And now, O gracious and blessed God,
Father, Son and Holy Spirit, thou art mine and I am thine.
So be it.
And the covenant which I have made on earth,
let it be ratified in heaven.
Amen.

The Servant of the Refugee

Lord, clear my eyes that I may see
the suffering of the refugee.
Unstop my ears that I might hear
the cries of those in deep despair.
Release my fettered feet to tread
paths where I may some comfort spread.
Unbind my hands that they may move,
the fullness of your love to prove.
Unloose my tongue that I may seek
your words of hope and love to speak.
Lord, fill my heart that I might be
your servant to the refugee.

Refugee and Migrant Service, Aotearoa, New Zealand

Croatia. Arrival of victims of "ethnic cleansing" from northern Bosnia and Herzegovina, Gašinci Camp, Slavonia.

UNHCR / 24009 / 02.1994 / A. Hollman

A Prayer with Movement

Begin the movement prayer by standing together in a circle. Practise the movements first, then say the prayer all together.

God, you ask us to love one another
(arms stretched out, palms up, into centre of circle)
as much as we love ourselves.
(cross hands over own heart)
Sometimes we forget who is our neighbour,
(turn around so now facing outwards)
And we forget about loving.
(fold arms tightly, bow head down)
Help us to love one another as much as we love ourselves
(turn around, join hands)
And as much as you love us.
(lift arms up high, keeping hands joined)
Amen.

Alyson Huntly, Canada

Behind the Mist _
the Sun Waits

I believe that behind the mist the sun waits.
I believe that beyond the dark night it is raining stars.
I believe in secret volcanoes and the world below.
I believe that this lost ship will reach port.
They will not rob me of hope, it shall not be broken.
My voice is filled to overflowing
    with the desire to sing, the desire to sing.
I believe in reason, and not in the force of arms;
I believe that peace will be sown throughout the
earth.
I believe in our nobility, created in the image of God,
    and with free will reaching for the skies.
They will not rob me of hope, it shall not be broken,
    it shall not be broken.

Chile. *Confessing Our Faith Around the World IV*, South America, World Council of Churches, 1985

A Prayer for Change

God our Creator,

As we join the large spectrum of Christians in different churches
who are praying for refugees, we realize that we are,
in fact, asking for changes in our own society.

We pray for politicians,
that they may be willing to share the prosperity
of our country with all people —
not only with their own citizens.
Send them someone who will give a name
and a human face to the refugee problem,
and thus show them the inhumanity of the legislation.

We pray for journalists and other who work in the media,
and thus influence public opinion.
Send into their experience events
which will safeguard them from cynicism
and invite them to use their capacities
to generate a friendlier atmosphere toward refugees.

We pray for the police and immigration officers at our airports,
who exercise power over the lives of people —
often without a real knowledge of their situation.
Send into their lives people who are able to help them
understand the reality of the asylum seekers.

We pray for ordinary citizens in our country,
that we may not be naive or indifferent,
but join those who are working
to alleviate the lot of refugees.

Finland. From *With All God's People: The New Ecumenical Prayer Circle* compiled by John
Carden. Geneva: WCC Publications, 1989.

God, our Creator,
        have mercy on us;
        we, who are acting as if freedom, peace
        and the well-being of our country
        were meant for our benefit alone.

God, our Creator,
        help us to become changed people,
        and to change our attitudes,
        as well as our legislation. Amen.

Thailand. Laotian hill tribe refugees, Chiang Kham Camp.

UNHCR / 18142 / 11.1988 / A. Hollmann

Leader: As they face this day, O God,
find those who are lost,
separated from those they love,
crossing unknown borders,
without a country or home,
not knowing where to turn:

People: *Find them, God who always seeks for the lost,*
and cover them safely as a hen covers her chickens.

Leader: As they face this day, O God,
stand among the ones in refugee camps around the world,
in the hunger and despair,
in the crowds and the emptiness,
in the wet and the thirstiness:

People: *Be their hope and their strength*
in the crying out for justice
and open the ears of the world to hear their cries.

Leader: As they face this day, O God,
may those who live with us,
    uprooted from their homelands,
find a new home
where their history is respected,
    their gifts and graces celebrated
and their fear departed form them.

People: *May we be their home,*
may we be the ones who open our hearts in welcome.

From the *Liturgy for Human Rights Sunday* prepared by the Christian Conference of Asia and the Uniting Church in Australia, October, 1996.

Leader: As we face this day, O God,
                sing to us your song of encouragement,
                paint for us your bright pictures of a new world
                where people need not flee from wars and oppression,
                where no one lacks a country or a home.
                and where we are all part of your new creation.

People: *For we long to be your people, in spirit and in truth.*
                We pray in the name of Jesus the Christ,
                who knew the life of a refugee.
                Amen.

My Mother had to go to Los Angeles

My mother had to go to Los Angeles because she could not find work to help our family survive. She went with my youngest brother. My grandmother looks after me and my four brothers and sisters. I carry my mother's picture everywhere. I miss my mother so much. Sometimes when I am alone I talk to her as though she was right here with me. I hope to become a nurse when I finish high school but above all I dream of the day when I can be reunited with my mother and brother. I feel alone. I want to feel like I belong to somebody.

Guatemalan child of woman labour migrant in the United States. From *A Moment to Choose: Risking to be with Uprooted Peoples*, a resource book produced by the World Council of Churches, 1996.

Praying for a _
Disarmed Heart

Here the Jewish tradition, opening with the Hebrew Bible, lends its unique voice to this Jubilee collection of Christian prayer. Our human longings know no boundaries: whether for appreciation of our common humanity, for the nurture of our children, or for God's healing presence.

> Is not this the fast that I choose:
> to loose the bonds of injustice,
> to undo the thongs of the yoke.
> Is it not to share your bread with the hungry,
> and not to hide yourself from your own kin?

— Isaiah 58:6, 8 —

When is it?

An old rabbi once asked his pupils how they could tell when the night had ended and the day had begun.

"Could it be," asked one student, "when you can see an animal in the distance and tell whether it's a sheep or a dog?"

"No," answered the rabbi.

Another asked, "Is it when you can look at a tree in the distance and tell whether it's a fig tree or a peach tree?"

"No," answered the rabbi.

"Then when is it?" the pupils demanded.

"It is when you can look on the face of any woman or man and see that it is your sister or brother. Because if you cannot see this, it is still night."

Tales of the Hasidim

Used with permission. Text from *For the Healing of the Nations*, Church World Service Office on Global Education (OGE), 2115 N. Charles Street, Baltimore, MD 21218-5755; phone 410-727-6106; fax: 410-727-6108.

Prayer

Ah yes, God of Sarah and Abraham!
That I may see!
That the eyes of my heart be enlightened,
    as St. Paul prayed for the Ephesians.
That I may, as Isaiah bids me,
    "not hide myself from my kin."
The Talmud's prescription is a single line:
urging that I avoid doing to my sister or brother
    what is hateful to me.
"That is the entire Law, all the rest is commentary."
In your infinite power,
    create in me a disarmed heart, O God!
May it be so.

___ Prayer from Mozambique __

You Made a Brother of a Stranger

Lord, today you made us known to friends we did not know,
And you have given us seats in homes which are not our own.
You have brought the distant near,
and made a brother of a stranger.
We thank you, Lord;
your love be praised.

Prayer from Mozambique, excerpt from *World Hunger Resource: Gleaning of Spirit*, produced by the Church World Service Office on Global Education (OGE), Baltimore, MD.

Bosnia and Herzegovina. Internally displaced woman, Tuzla Airbase, anxiously awaits news of relative in Srebrenica.

UNHCR / 25105 / 08.1995 / R. LeMoyne

A Creed

We believe in a community that opens its doors
        to people who flee war, hunger and poverty
        in search of a better life.

We believe in the power of love, not the power of violence.

We believe that we are called to share our lives
        so as to free each other from poverty, racism
        and oppression of all kinds.

We believe that the resources of the earth
        are to be shared among all people —
        not just the few.

We believe in a community that has as a priority
        a response to those who are denied
        basic human rights and dignity.

We reject a world where people are denied access to warmth,
        food, shelter and the right to live in peace.

We want to believe in justice, in goodness and in people.

We believe we are called to a life of freedom,
        of service,
        of witness,
        of hope.

We reject the idea that nothing can be done.

We believe that a time will come when all people
        will share in the richness of our world,
        and that all people will be truly loved and respected.

From *Stay With Us: Worship Resources*, CAFOD, London, England.

We commit ourselves in the name of God
who created the world for all to share,
of Christ who leads us to freedom, and
of the Spirit who calls us to action.

Today we commit ourselves to work together
to make this belief a reality.

Pakistan. Afghan refugee awaits international aid.

UNHCR / 11117 / S. Errington

Litany Protecting __

Human Life and Dignity

Leader: Let us now place ourselves in the presence
            of Jesus Christ our Lord
      and remember with sorrow
      our many faults and weaknesses.

      Let us pause for a silent reflection.

      Lord Jesus, you demand from us a life freed
            from selfishness and self-seeking.
      Forgive us for the times when we have tried
            to dominate and exploit our fellow human beings.

People: ***Lamb of God, you take away the sins of the world,
      have mercy on us.***

Leader: Lord Jesus, you demand from us a respect
            for the dignity and rights of each and every one
            of our fellow human beings.
      Forgive us for the times when we have
            treated others unjustly,
            and have failed to stand up for others
            when their rights were violated.

People: ***Lamb of God, you take away the sins of the world,
      have mercy on us.***

Leader: Lord Jesus, you demand from us openness
            and generosity to anyone in need,
            including strangers and even those
            we considered to be our enemies.

Prepared by the Committee for the Week of Prayer and Confession in Africa, which was marked June 16–23, 1966.

Forgive us for the times when we have
closed our hearts and minds
to your example and your will.

People: ***Lamb of God, you take away the sins of the world,
have mercy on us.***

Leader: Let us now turn to God, our loving Father,
and say the prayer that the Lord Jesus taught us:

The Lord's Prayer

Blanca

Blanca is a tiny woman from the Central American nation El Salvador. In a betrayal of its sacred name, this country has been, for many of its citizens, an instrument of torture and death rather than a land of salvation and life. Blanca's husband was murdered by the military authorities because of his union activities. Her grief was quickly followed by fear as she sensed that she was being followed. She decided to leave her home, taking with her only her most precious possessions — her children.

By bus and on foot, she had crossed the entire North American continent to seek safe haven in Canada – a country she had heard was kind to refugees. Now she sat in my office with her three-year-old son and one-and-a-half year old twins, telling me her story.

Courageous, determined, resourceful and devoted to her children.

Divided by many kilometres and many centuries, Blanca is a modern Ruth. Her life, and the lives of the many other women and children which each of you could share, bland together to be the prophetic witness that has nourished and challenged the church since the beginning of creation.

Told by Rev. Glynnis Williams, Action Réfugiés, Montreal, Canada

Prayer of

Thanksgiving and Confession

Today, Gracious God,
>we worship you are the one born among us:
>born, like many refugees, in makeshift conditions,
>surviving amidst bloodshed and terror,
>forced to leave your place of birth
>>and go to a foreign land.

Born as one of us, we worship you, Refugee God.

Today, Gracious God,
>we worship you as one forced to flee from danger,
>avoiding those with murderous intent,
>finding a home far away from the centre of worship
>>and action.

Born as one of us, we worship you, Refugee God.

Today, Gracious God,
>we worship you as one who lived with those
>>forced to the edges,
>as one who taught and demonstrated
>the great depth of love you have for each person,
>whether homeless or stateless.

Born as one of us, we worship you, loving God.

We thank you for the wisdom of strangers from the east
>who found and worshipped you in a stable,
>>and we thank you for the faith of the Syrophonecian
>>woman who extended your mission.

Refugee and Migrant Service, Aotearoa, New Zealand.

We confess we are not always open
to the wisdom strangers bring.

We do not seek to live amongst those whose lives are disrupted.

We give importance to status and grandeur.

Forgive us.

We thank you for your graciousness.

You continually come to us
speaking words of love and forgiveness.

Thanks be to God.

Amen.

Somalia. Ethiopian refugee, Gannet Camp.

UNHCR / 15069 / C. Berger

Prayer of Intercession
for Women and Children

Spirit of Life, we remember today the women,
    named and unnamed,
    who throughout time have used the power and gifts
    you gave them to change the world.
    We call upon these foremothers
    to help us discover within ourselves your power —
    and the ways to use it to bring about
        the Reign of Justice and Peace.

We remember Sarah
    who with Abraham answered God's call
    to forsake her homeland and
    put their faith in a covenant with the Lord.

    We pray for her power of faith.

We remember Esther and Deborah,
    who by acts of individual courage saved their nation.

    We pray for their power of courage
    to act for the greater good.

We remember Mary Magdalene,
    and the other women who followed Jesus
    who were not believed when they announced the resurrection.

    We pray for their power of belief
    in the face of skepticism.

Adapted from Ann M. Heidkamp, "A Litany for Many Voices." From the worship book used at the consultation The Prophetic Mission of Churches in Response to Forced Displacement of People held in Addis Ababa, Ethiopia, November 1995, co-sponsored by Caritas Internationalis, Lutheran World Federation/World Service, and the World Council of Churches.

We pray for the millions of children and women
who face a life of poverty and malnutrition.

*May they be granted the power of hopefulness
to work together for a better life.*

We pray for those women who have been forced
to leave their homes and their communities
and who struggle to reconstruct their worlds
and their lives.

May they have the courage to begin anew.

We pray for uprooted children
whose lives have been turned upside down
by forces beyond their control.

*May they feel your comfort and guidance
as they struggle to grow up in unfamiliar worlds.*

Amen.

Irish Blessing

May the blessing of light be on you,
    light without and light within.
May the blessed sunlight shine upon you
    and warm your heart
    till it glows like a great fire,
    and strangers may warm themselves
    as well as friends.
And may the light shine out of the eyes of you
    like a candle set
    in the window of a house,
    bidding the wanderer to come in
    out of the storm.
May you ever have a kindly greeting for people
    as you're going along the roads.
And now may the Lord bless you,
    and bless you kindly,
Amen.

British Council of Churches.

A Closing Prayer

Leader: Give us, O Lord, churches in our societies:

People: that will be more courageous than cautious,
that will not merely "comfort the afflicted
but afflict the comfortable."

Leader: Give us, O Lord, churches in our societies:

People: that will not only love the world
but will also judge the world,
that will not only pursue peace
but also demand justice.

Leader: Give us, O Lord, churches in our societies:

People: that will not remain silent
when people are calling for a voice,
that will not pass by on the other side
when wounded humanity is waiting to be healed.

Leader: Give us, O Lord, churches in our societies:

People: that not only call us to worship
but also send us out to witness,
that will follow Christ
even when the way points to a cross.

All: *To this end, we offer ourselves*
in the name of Him who loved us
and gave Himself for us. Amen.

From "Becoming a Church of the Stranger," a Bible study produced by the Christian Conference of Asia, June, 1997.

Worship
Services
&
Liturgies

Working for __
Peace and Justice

In this worship, we commit ourselves to working for a more just and peaceful world — a world where people are not forced from their communities and where they live in peace and harmony with one another.

Greeting

Leader: I will light a light
in the name of God
who lit the world
and breathed the breath of life into me.
I will light a light
in the name of the Son
who saved the world
and stretched out his hand to me.
I will light a light
in the name of the Spirit
who encompasses the world
and blesses my soul with yearning.

All: We will light three lights for the trinity of love:
God above us,
God beside us,
God beneath us:
the beginning,
the end,
the everlasting one.
Amen.

From the worship book used at the consultation The Prophetic Mission of Churches in Response to Forced Displacement of People held in Addis Ababa, Ethiopia, November 1995, co-sponsored by Caritas Internationalis, Lutheran World Federation/World Service, and the World Council of Churches.

Song

Prayer

Plant us, God, deep in the soil of your word.
Nurture us with the water of baptism
so that we may flourish in your presence
always producing the fruits of your compassion
and growing in you and towards one another.
Then we will be steadfast and sure,
sheltering all your people with life and love,
through Jesus Christ, who reigns with you and the Holy Spirit
one God, now and forever. Amen.

Entrance of the Word

Scripture readings

> Jeremiah 6:13–14
> Luke 4:16–21

Message

Song

Prayers of Intercession

O God of peace, we pray for the victims of wars —
> in Rwanda and Bosnia, in Afghanistan and a dozen
> other places where people suffer the ravages of violence,

> *Lord, have mercy.*

O God, our loving parent, we pray for migrant workers
> who are forced to work in far-away countries
> in order to provide for their families.

> *Lord, have mercy.*

O God of understanding, we pray for all those who live
> in precarious situations, whose societies are marked
> by oppression and tension and who may one day
> be uprooted from their communities,

> *Lord, have mercy.*

O God, the creator of our wondrous world,
>   we pray for our fragile environment —
>   for the animals and trees, the water and the soil itself
>   which has suffered as a result of our greed
>   and inattention and which too often can no longer
>   sustain human life.

> **Lord, have mercy.**

O God, we ask you to make us more effective advocates
>   for peace and justice. Give us the creativity, compassion
>   and the endurance to build a better world,
>   where people will not have to abandon their homes
>   and communities and where all will live in peace,
>   justice and harmony with each other
>   and with nature which sustains us all.

> **Lord, have mercy.**

Response

Reflection

Prayer of Commitment

Sisters and brothers,
>   let us stand and affirm what we have discovered
>   of God's will in the company of each other.
That we worship one God,
>   Father, Son and Holy Spirit,
>   in whose image we are made,
>   to whose service we are summoned,
>   by whose presence we are renewed,

This we believe.

That it is central to the mission of Christ
>   to participate, by word and action,
>   in the struggles of the poor for justice,
>   to share justly the earth's land and resources,
>   to rejoice in the diversity of human culture,
>   to preserve human life in all its beauty and frailty,

to accompany the uprooted and to welcome the stranger,
and to witness — every day —
to the love of God for people of the earth,

This we believe.

That we are called to become the Church of the Stranger,
    to open ourselves to the transforming power
        of the Holy Spirit
    which may come to us through the foreigner,
    to take the risk of speaking out on behalf of those
        who are different from us,
    and to see that when we minister to the stranger,
        the uprooted,
    we are serving our Lord and Saviour.

This we believe.

That God has called the church into being
    to be the servant of the kingdom,
    to be a sign of God's new order,
    to celebrate in the streets and fields of every land
        the liturgy of heaven,

This we believe.

That Christ, fully aware of our differences,
    prays that we might be one
    so that the world may believe

This we believe.

and to this we are committed
    for the love of God,
    in the way of Christ,
    by the power of the Holy Spirit. Amen.

Benediction

O God, help us to persevere without stress,
   to achieve without success,
   to arrive without striving,
so that all that we do
   brings glory to you.
Amen.

Closing Hymn

I Want to Go Home
A Liturgy for Human Rights Sunday

Hear the cries of the uprooted peoples
around the world.

Leader: Today we celebrate Human Rights Sunday with a focus on the uprooted people in the world, especially those who have fled their countries and have become refugees or those who have been forced to live like refugees in their own land.

Let us call into this worship the presence of friends, companions and people whom we respect from around the world:
- those whose rights have been violated;
- those who worked hard and risked their lives that the rights of others may be respected;
- those who have walked towards the coming of God's kingdom of justice, peace and wholeness of life;
- those who have been uprooted from their land due to war, conflict and the destruction of their environment.

There is no place where you cannot reach:

People: *God who made the heavens and the earth.*

Leader: There is no journey which you have not traveled:

People: *God who shared our life in Jesus Christ.*

From the *Liturgy for Human Rights Sunday* prepared by the Christian Conference of Asia and the Uniting Church in Australia, October, 1996.

Leader: There are no people beyond your care:

People: *God who is the Spirit, the Comforter.*
          Let us worship God!

Hymn

Gather Them In

Leader: Let us "gather in" to our community of faith
          some of the people who are uprooted from
          their homes and countries around the world.

The names of countries where there are known to be refugees or where there are known to be internally displaced could be read and flowers placed on the table for them, or candles lit, or a ribbon attached to the map linked with the congregation or the communion table.

Testimonies/stories of uprooted peoples

Select from stories [in this book] or ask local refugee people or those coming from internally displaced communities to share their stories.

Leader: As we gather together in this place, we remember these
          people and the struggle of their lives.

People: *We will remember them before our God.*
          It is not easy to welcome everyone

Leader: Even when we hope we can do better,
          it is not easy to welcome everyone
          that wants to live among us,
          or need our prayers and concerned support, O God.
          There are many reasons why we find it hard:

The people say why it is hard.

OR

Voice 1: Sometimes we feel people are very different from us,
          in culture, in looks, in ways of relating,
          in their politics, in their religion;

Voice 2: Or we feel as though there is not enough to share
with them in work, in houses, in schools,
in money, in services;

Voice 3: Sometimes we are tired
and cannot find the energy to give the care,
or the time that they may hope from us,
especially when they are far away.

All: Forgive us, O God,
if we have been less than generous.
We remember your grace in relating to us
and we long to be as gracious to others.

Assurance

Leader: Our prayers are heard.
From the Spirit, have we all received,
grace upon grace.

People: Thanks be to God!

Readings

Suggested Readings

Isaiah 49:8–21 *(or part of)*; Psalm 124
1 Corinthians 4:8–13; Matthew 25:31–46 *(or part of)*

Hymn

Sermon

Affirmation of faith

See page 11.

Offering

To be accompanied by music from another country.
The offering is received.

Leader: Dear God, receive our offering.
Guide those who use it that it may help to bring
fullness of life to those who live in need
and long for our care.

People: Amen.

Intercession

See page 29.

The Lord's Prayer

Hymn

Blessing and Dismissal

Leader: Go in peace and grace.
And may God lift up new possibilities before us,
the face of Christ be seen in our neighbours
and the Spirit lead us into the celebration
of a new community.

People: *Amen.*

*Somalia.
Ethiopian refugees
at Bo'o Camp get
drinking water.*

UNHCR / 12128 / Y. Müller

Because Christ died for me,
I have been redeemed and I am part of his great family.
Everywhere in the world I am at home, because I am with my
brothers and sisters.
I know my brothers and sisters need me, so that they too can be
at home everywhere.
I believe with them that Christ came
to fulfil the promise of grace.

— Isaiah 61:2 —

I commit myself to Christ, that all things may be made new.

— Revelation 21:5 —

Invocation

For surely I know the plans I have for you, says the Lord,
        plans for your welfare and not for harm,
        to give you a future with hope.
Then when you call upon me and come and pray to me;
        I will hear you.
When you search for me, you will find me;
        if you seek for me with all your heart,
        I will let you find me, says the Lord.

— Jeremiah 29:11–14 —

Prepared by the Committee for the Week of Prayer and Confession in Africa, which was marked June 16–23, 1996.

Confession of Sins

Father, far from having dominion over creation,
    we have let ourselves be dominated by it.
Far from guarding and cultivating it,
    we have exploited and destroyed it
Your word is not enough for us, we look for proof.
We jealously hoard what we call "ours,"
    even though it is a gift from you.
We proclaim the gospel badly,
    because we expect from the start that it will not be heard.
We rely on our own strength, our intelligence, our faith,
    instead of being open to receive your command.
We are afraid of suffering for your word, so we keep silent.
We do not believe that the nations will come to you,
    and we say to you, "send someone else…"
When war has broken out we have not given
    our uprooted brother or sister shelter in our homes.
We have contributed to conflicts through our indifference
        or our reluctance to intervene to establish
            or re-establish the conditions for lasting peace.
Lord, in your goodness,
        forgive us we pray and through your Holy Spirit,
        use us nonetheless for the fulfillment of your promise
        in Jesus Christ.
O Lord, our God, in whom we have our hope.
Amen.

Words of Hope

In the depths of exile, a people in captivity receives a message:
        I will give you a future with hope.
        When the future is bleak,
        When hope has broken down,
A people receives a promise:
        You will pray to me and I will hear you.
        When God is hidden and silent,
A people receives assurance:

Seek me and you will find me.
We praise and bless you
> for your word in the midst of our silence,
> for your faithfulness in our erring ways,
> for your light in our darkness
> for your faith in the midst of our unbelief.

We praise and bless you,
> for your fountain in our deserts,
> for your life in our graveyards
> for your presence in our exiles,
> for your breath upon our clay.

We praise and bless you
> for your victory over our anxieties,
> for your bread in our loneliness,
> for your gospel on our wounds,
> for your resurrection in our brokenness. Amen.

Prayer of Intercession

Leader: Let us pray for the uprooted people in our countries.

(silent prayer)

People: ***In your great mercy, grant these uprooted people hope in your promise of a new world. In the name of the Father, the Son and the Holy Spirit. Amen.***

Leader: Let us prayer for the uprooted people in Africa.

(silent prayer)

People: ***In your great mercy, grant these uprooted people hope in your promise of a new world. In the name of the Father, the Son and the Holy Spirit. Amen.***

Leader: Let us pray for the uprooted people in the world.

(silent prayer)

People: ***In your great mercy, grant these uprooted people hope in your promise of a new world. In the name of the Father, the Son and the Holy Spirit. Amen.***

Liturgy on the Theme
of Uprooted People

Assembly to form two circles, one inner circle and one outer circle. Members are invited to read the responses according to the circle they are in.

Outer Circle:

> God, bless our feet
> which have journeyed for so many miles.
> Will they take us down the right path to safety,
> to a new place to call home?

Inner Circle:

> Lord, give our feet strength
> to accompany our brothers and sisters
> who have been uprooted from their homelands.

OC:

> God, bless our legs.
> We have been told to wait, told to stand,
> told to move as we are in the wrong line.
> Come back tomorrow, they say, to wait.

IC:

> Lord, give our legs strength
> to stand in solidarity,
> to stand alongside those people
> who are waiting to find a safe place to rest.

OC:

> God, bless our stomachs,
> knotted in anger and fear, hunger and illness.

By Beverly O'Grady, a part-time theological student, a catechist at St. Dominic's Catholic Church, Mississauga, Ontario, Canada, and a staff member of The United Church of Canada's Division of World Outreach.

IC: Lord, give us strength
        to stomach the injustices we must see
        in order to recognize them
        and not to turn away to ease our own discomfort.

OC: God, bless our arms
        as they bear the weight of our few possessions
        and the small children that we must carry.

IC: Lord, give our arms strength
        to reach out to the newcomer,
        making each one welcome.

OC: God, bless our hands,
        which are cracked and bleeding
        from the endless search to find work,
            to find food,
        to hold onto those few strands of our former lives.

IC: Lord, give our hands strength
        to work for justice and righteousness.

OC: God, bless our mouths
        as we continue to ask endless questions.
        Where can we go to find peace?
        Where can we find our mothers,
            fathers,
            spouses,
            our children?
        Who can tell us where to go next?

IC: Lord, open our mouths
        to speak words of kindness to the newcomer,
        to demand justice for all people,
        to defend those most in need.

OC: God, bless our ears
        so they will be ready to hear the many instructions
            in foreign languages.

IC: Lord, open our ears
        to hear your words
        as spoken by the lonely and oppressed.

OC: God, bless our heads,
        so tired from thinking what to do next,
        where to go next,
        how to learn yet another language,
        to learn the rules of another country's bureaucracy.

IC: Lord, help us to recognize the Christ in each one of us.

Personal Blessing

Members of the inner circle will turn to face those of the outer circle, each taking a turn to offer a personal prayer, by making a small sign of blessing over each others' eyes, ears, mouth, shoulders and hands while saying the following prayer:

I bless your eyes so that you will recognize injustices.
I bless your ears so you will hear the cry of the stranger.
I bless your mouth so that you will speak words of welcome
        to newcomers.
I bless your shoulders so you will be able to bear the weight
        of struggling for justice.
I bless your hands so that you can work together with all people
        to establish peace.
Amen.

Sharing the Pain ___
of the Uprooted

I n this worship, we express our solidarity with those who have been uprooted from their homes and communities — like trees which have been torn from their soil.

Greeting

The grace of the Lord Jesus Christ, the love of God and the communion of the Holy Spirit be with you all.

All: *And also with you.*

Leader: Let us praise God, who gives living water,
           through whom the faithful flourish.
      Like trees planted by the water, God,
           are those who trust in you.
      Like trees with deep roots
           are those who place their faith in you.
      Like green trees in winter
           are those who receive their life from you.

All: *We praise you, God, for life that has no end,*
        through Jesus our risen Christ.

Song

From the worship book used at the consultation The Prophetic Mission of Churches in Response to Forced Displacement of People held in Addis Ababa, Ethiopia, November 1995, co-sponsored by Caritas Internationalis, Lutheran World Federation/World Service, and the World Council of Churches.

Prayer

How can we sing your song, O God, in a strange land?
How can we witness to your all-embracing love
    with lives full of painful contradictions?
How can we be ambassadors of reconciliation
    in a world enslaved by sin and death,
      where children suffer and starve,
      and many labour in vain while a few live in luxury;
      where in the midst of our lives,
      we dwell under the shadow of death?
What answer shall we give to the suffering
    (what shall we say to our own hearts)
      when they cry from the depths: "Where is now your God?"

Response

A Lament

Remember, O Lord, what has befallen us,
    look, and see our disgrace.
Our inheritance has been turned over to strangers,
    our homes to aliens.
We have become orphans, fatherless;
    our mothers are like widows.
We must pay for the water we drink;
    the wood we get must be bought.
With a yoke on our necks we are hard driven;
    we are weary, we are given no rest

— Lamentations 5:1–5 —

An uprooted one from Eritrea says:

"I returned to my village after 17 years. There was nothing left. The stream we used to play in as children was dry. The lake was dry. There were no trees left. There were no homes left."

Response

> Blindly they wandered through the streets,
> so defiled with blood
> that no one was able to touch their garments.
> "Away! Unclean!" people shouted at them;
> "Away! Away! Do not touch!"
> So they became fugitives and wanderers;
> it was said among the nations,
> "They shall stay here no longer."

— Lamentations 4:14–15 —

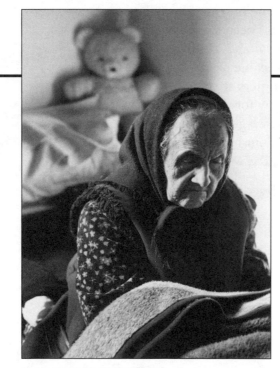

Croatia. Some elderly refugees arrive on their own from northern Bosnia and Herzegovina, Gašinci Camp, Slavonia.

UNHCR / 24012 / 02.1994 / A. Hollmann

An uprooted one in Britain says:

> "I can't bear this life of hiding any more. They say I am not a refugee, but I know I will be imprisoned, tortured, killed if I return. They ask for proof. I worry about my wife and children back home. Is there anyone who cares?"

Response

> My eyes will flow without ceasing, without respite,
>   until the Lord from heaven looks down and sees.
> My eyes cause me grief
>   at the fate of all the young women in my city.

> — Lamentations 3:49–51 —

An uprooted one, a domestic worker from Hong Kong, says:

> "I cry every night when I go to bed…no woman should be faced with such a choice…. Parents don't know how lucky they are to be able to kiss and hug their children every day…. My employers don't even know that I am a mother."

Response

> Is it nothing to you, all who pass by?
> Look and see if there is any sorrow like this sorrow.

> — Lamentations 1:12, adapted —

Silence

Prayer of Intercession

We pray for all of those who are uprooted,
   who are hunted, who are fleeing for their lives,
   and who so often find only closed borders,
      closed doors, and closed faces.

We pray for the women and men, the children and the elderly
   who seek to find safety and solace
   and who yearn to begin new lives.

We pray for those who pass by,
    who would rather not hear the pleading or see the fear
    or recognize the human being in need of help.

Leader: Too many times the uprooted are invisible and name-
    less. As we close this prayer of intercession, we invite
    you each to write the name of an uprooted person on a
    piece of paper and to come forward and place that name
    on this uprooted tree. Let us sing as we place our names
    on the tree and as we pray to God for mercy.

    Oh God of mercy and compassion,
    we lift up the names of these our brothers and sisters
    who have been forced to leave their communities
    and we lift up the millions of other uprooted people
    in this world whose names we don't know,
    but who are known to you.
    Be with them, Oh God,
    and also with us as we struggle to do your will.
    We pray to you, oh God,
    in the words of your son, Jesus Christ.

Lord's Prayer

Prayer of Commitment

Open my eyes that they may see the deepest needs
    of men and women;
Move my hands that they may feed the hungry.
Touch my heart that it may bring warmth to the despairing;
Teach me the generosity that welcomes strangers;
Let me share my possessions to clothe the naked;
Give me the care that strengthens the sick;
Make me share in the quest to set the prisoners free;
In sharing our anxiety and our love,
our poverty and our prosperity,
we partake of your divine presence. Amen.

Canaan Banana, Zimbabwe

Benediction

Leader: May the love of the Lord Jesus draw you to himself:
           May the power of the Lord Jesus strengthen you
               in his service.
           May the joy of the Lord Jesus fill your spirit
           And the blessing of God Almighty,
               the Father, the Son and the Holy Spirit,
               be upon you and remain with you forever.
           Amen.

Uprooted Peoples ___
A Worship Outline

At various points in this outline, it is suggested that participants move to another seat or location beside another person, perhaps someone they do not know, to simulate having no lasting home (Hebrews 13:14). You may use or ignore this suggestion. It is marked each time with an (*).

Gathering the People

Preface

First Reader:

> We are now a church of strangers.
>
> Konrad Raiser, Secretary General of the
World Council of Churches

> Our congregations, like our neighbourhoods, are in constant flux. We promise at baptism to care for a child who, a year later, moves to some distant city.

Second Reader:

> We are now a race of travellers
> ranging wide o'er earth's whole face,
> every state is now our village,
> every town our marketplace.
>
> Derwyn Dixon Jones, *The Hymn Book*, 222

Opening Hymn* *(during which people may choose to move)*

Quiet Reflection

Worshippers are asked to close their eyes, and meditate as in a prayer, moving mentally into another space, while the following is read.

By David Allan, a United Church of Canada minister. From *Mandate Special Edition*, April 1997, The United Church of Canada.

First Reader:

Humanity is on the move, not always willingly. Today, it is estimated there are 20 million refugees in the world. The hills are alive with the sound of people's tramping feet, travelling someplace else.

That figure represents only refugees. What about those displaced by the closing of the fishery in Newfoundland? Or the mother and child seeking refuge at the Red Door Shelter in Toronto after being evicted from their apartment? Or the teenager on Grenville Street in Vancouver huddled in a doorway for the night, asking for change from passers-by?

Aboriginal peoples have been forced by governments to move from one place to another in the Soviet Union and Australia and Canada. Senior citizens are moved by families into institutions or to other towns away from familiar surroundings and friends.

Second Reader:

The Ramishams came to Canada from Guyana, worked hard, saw their son graduate from university last year. But the only job he could find is in Korea. In two generations, they have moved between three continents. Louise is a fifth generation Quebecker who has left her ancestral province for Alberta. People in urban and suburban areas find their neighbourhoods are populated by people from around the world.

Remembering the Stories

Readings from Scripture

Choose which scripture(s) you wish to read. The background notes can be read before the scripture text.

Exodus 2:11–12, 15, 23 to 3:5, 7, 10–14

Moses is displaced in the Midian wilderness, without the usual supports of family, position, and community. Who is he now? In his strange encounter with God in the burning bush he asked God's name. The answer is: "I Am

Who I Am." That is what every uprooted stranger comes to realize—you only bring yourself. In the answer "I Am Who I Am," God is identified as displaced and lost and alone. God's response is not a deep, philosophical reply. It is the word of a refugee in a foreign place. It is the word of a God who is a stranger, too.

Deuteronomy 26:5–11

Thought by many to contain the remnants of the oldest creed in all scripture, this passage begins with the confession of the uprooted: "A wandering Aramean was my father…"

Genesis 11:31

The story of Abraham, which begins at this passage, starts in the valley of the Euphrates where his father takes a notion to emigrate far to the north, and ends up in Haran. His son later goes south from there into the Palestinian plain, and even as far south as Egypt. Poor Sarah seems dragged along by these wandering males. Home is on the road.

Ruth 1:1–22

Ruth was a Moabite, a people particularly hated by Israel, and a foreigner in Palestine. Yet she becomes the grandmother of Israel's greatest king, David, an ancestor of Jesus.

Psalm 137

Judah is conquered and taken into exile. Jerusalem is demolished and burned when Babylonian soldiers march. In this psalm we hear the sorrow and anger of the uprooted. Consider that much of the Hebrew Scripture (or Old Testament) and the institution of the synagogue was the result of the destruction of the familiar and beloved, the product of exile.

Matthew 2

Mary, Joseph and Jesus were forced to flee to Egypt as generations of Jews had done. It is from the Jewish exiles in Egypt that the Greek Old Testament emerged. This is the source that is always quoted by New Testament authors. And it is "from Egypt that I have called my son" that provides Matthew's motif for the new Israel. Matthew's Gospel was written in Syria for Christian refugees from Jerusalem.

Exodus 23:9

Romans 3 and 4

Paul takes the covenant with Abraham to be "the father of many nations" and applies it to the question of whether Gentiles can be Christians if they are not Jews. Paul is a radical interpreter and says the aliens are also members of God's promise. "Is God the God of the Jews only?" he asks in an argument that cuts to the quick. He stretches "many nations" to include the world.

Hebrews 10:32

The unknown author of Hebrews begins a masterful discussion of the identification of God with the uprooted in this passage. It lasts through chapter 11 *(you needn't read it all)* and climaxes with "here we have no continuing city, but we seek a city which is to come" in 13:14.

Other scripture notes:

Even the Eden story begins in paradise and ends in exile, homelessness, wandering. And the name by which Christians were known in Antioch suggests a people who are journeying. They are the people of The Way.

If you read more than one of these, you might have people move after each reading, or even stand, like the injunction to the Hebrews to stand while eating the Passover meal so that they'd be ready to go.

Hymn*

The Word Proclaimed

Breaking the Bread*

A bidding prayer, where each petition is followed by silence so the people can respond silently with their own prayer. (The stories are real, but the names are changed.)

Let us pray:

For people like Mary,
    a single mom who cannot pay the rent,
    looking for a hostel for her children and herself,
    hoping against hope she will not have to surrender custody,

    AND for Sam,
    the doctor from Bosnia,
    who has brought his wife and family to safety to Canada
    but cannot practise medicine here
    so works part time at a pizza place,

    AND for Mercy,
    in flight from other Christians in Rwanda
        of a different tribe;
    and for all those who journey
    with all that they can call their own
        on their bent backs, like a cross…

Let us pray:

For people like Jacob,
    his family's pride and joy and hope back in Ghana,
    who has somehow earned his university degree here in Canada
    in spite of impossible foreign student fees,
    by eating one meal a day for seven years
    and through menial part-time work, all alone;

    AND for Maria,
    the accountant from the Philippines
    who scrubs floors here so she can send money back home
    to Mindanao;

AND for Tommy,
the artist from Cape Breton who scrubs dishes
    in a downtown bar
because Sydney has no jobs for artists
    and neither does Toronto;
and for all whose hands bear the print of pain,
like nails…

Let us pray:

For people like Martha
    from a reserve in Manitoba
    who cries alone in her room in North Winnipeg
    for her children she cannot find any more;

AND for Terry,
    whose sexual orientation has made him
    an unwanted stranger to his family;
    and for all those whose faces bear the marks of grief and loss,
    like the traces of thorns…

Let us pray:

For people like Jennifer
    who is so tired of running
        from parents who assault her,

AND for Joanne,
    practising the sex trade to stay alive,

AND for Waleed,
    who escaped through the Turkish mountains from Iran
    because he wanted to become a Christian;
    and for all those whose feet are so sore from walking
    so far for so long
    on their own Via Dolorosa.

Let us pray:

For Richard,
    a gentle Ojibway in a prison far from home,
    frightened amongst violent men,
    who drank himself stupid because he was so homesick,

AND for Mabel
staring at the brown wall
in the impersonal blankness of her strange room
   at the Sunset Home
at the end of her days,

AND for Phil,
who never thought 20 years ago
that at 50 he'd be standing in an unemployment line;
and for all those who see the awful grin of inmates,
   matrons,
   and counsellors,
like their very own Place of the Skull…

For all these uprooted people
   crying in the night "Oh Jesus",
   we, too, pray "Oh Jesus"…
   Amen.

The Peace Of Christ*

Invite people to move about quietly shaking hands with others. Then pass around a chunk of break from which people can tear a piece symbolizing the food ration of refugees, of the unemployed, and of the hungry of all the world. (Note: This is not the Lord's Supper.) *You may say words such as: Food for the day, The bread of life, Our daily bread, or Take and eat.*

Reader:

   Let us remember the words of Jesus to uprooted people:

      Blessed are the poor (in spirit)
      for theirs is the kingdom of God.
      Blessed are those who mourn
      for they will be comforted.
      Blessed are the meek
      for they will inherit the earth.
  Blessed are those who hunger and thirst (for righteousness)
      for they will be filled…

Blessed are those who are persecuted...
for theirs is the kingdom of heaven...
Rejoice and be glad...
You are the salt of the earth...
You are the light of the world...

— from Matthew 5:3–14 —

(Bracketed parts may be omitted; Luke did!)

Hymn

Commissioning And Benediction

Go now into the world
    and the companionship of God go with you all the way.
Amen.

(Companion literally means "with bread" in its Latin root.)

___ Migrant Workers, Refugees, ___
Internally Displaced Peoples in Asia

Call to Worship

Modern Beatitudes

Jesus, is this what you say to us today?
How blest are those who abhor easy pieties
    the *kingdom* of heaven is theirs.
How blest are those who train in non-violence
    they shall have the earth for their possession.
How blest are those who fast for justice
    they shall be satisfied.
How blest are those who see enemies as human
    mercy shall be shown to them.
How blest are those who live what they profess
    they shall see God.
How blest are those who build bridges of reconciliation
    God shall call them friends.
How blest are those who show the outcast
      that someone understands
    the *kingdom* of heaven is theirs.

Silent Meditation

Candle is lit symbolising the voice of the migrant workers, refugees, and internally displaced peoples in Asia.

Hymn

From the Christian Conference of Asia consultation on migrant workers, refugees and internally displaced in Asia, Oct. 1995.

Prayer of Confession and Commitment

Leader: We are here to listen and to learn
from stories
from situations
from facts and figures …
from the voices that cry for our attention.

People: *Forgive us, God of all peoples,*
for those times we have chosen not to listen
to the voices
and chosen not to learn from their stories.

Leader: We hear the cries of the people —
their cries for dignity, hope, freedom to be.

People: *Forgive us if we, the church,*
through our inattention and our fears,
have added to their pain and despair
of being strangers in an unknown land.

Leader: When they feel demoralized through lack of support

People: *May we impart strength.*

Leader: When hopelessness drowns their dreams and
loneliness is their only companion

People: *May we affirm their right to be*
and impart hope and warmth.

Leader: God of all peoples, empower the church that
We may hear
may listen
may act
and that we may risk ourselves to be the voice of those
whose voices are overpowered by the clamour of today's
world.

Silence

All: *Loving God,*
who calls the church
to be the church of the stranger
Enable us to hear
Enable us to listen
Empower us to act.

Scripture Reading

Leviticus 19:33 and 34

Meditation

Response of Faith

Voices 1: We are called to be the church
the witness of Christ in the world
the disciples who follow in the steps
of the one who lived within and for the marginalized —
those kept to the outside of society.
We are called to welcome the stranger in our midst.

Voices 2: But our hospitality is hindered by our anxieties.
Our open arms are closed by our fears.
Stir within us the flame of solidarity
so that we will commit ourselves to action,
That by our thoughts, our words, our dreams
the strangers in our midst will find their home.

Sending Forth

As we go now to our work together:
We go with the strength that is ours
We go simply
lightly
gently
in search of love and truth
And the Spirit goes with us.
Amen.

Recognizing the Strength
of Women and Children

In this worship, we lift up the strengths of women and children who make up the majority of the world's uprooted and who struggle to recreate and to nurture families and communities in new surroundings.

Greeting

In the midst of hunger and war
> we celebrate the promise of plenty and peace.

In the midst of oppression and tyranny
> we celebrate the promise of service and freedom.

In the midst of doubt and despair
> we celebrate the promise of faith and hope,

In the midst of fear and betrayal
> we celebrate the promise of joy and loyalty.

In the midst of hatred and death
> we celebrate the promise of love and life.

In the midst of sin and decay
> we celebrate the promise of salvation and renewal.

In the midst of death on every side
> we celebrate the promise of the living Christ.

From the worship book used at the consultation The Prophetic Mission of Churches in Response to Forced Displacement of People held in Addis Ababa, Ethiopia, November 1995, co-sponsored by Caritas Internationalis, Lutheran World Federation/World Service, and the World Council of Churches.

Prayer

Healer of nations,
you welcome all people and bid us to do the same
Speak clearly to us, "come to me, all you that are weary
and are carrying heavy burdens,
and I will give you rest."

— based on Matthew 11:28–29 —

O God, hear us, hear our prayer.

True vine,
we are the branches, abide in us as we abide in you,
so that we bear much fruit.
Speak clearly to us
"Love one another as I have loved you."

— John 15:5, 12 adapted —

O God, hear us, hear our prayer.

Tree of Life,
you give a garland instead of ashes,
the oil of gladness instead of mourning.
Speak clearly to us, "For as the earth brings forth its shoots,
and as a garden causes what is sown in it to spring up,
so the Lord God will cause righteousness and praise
to spring up before all the nations."

— based on Isaiah 61:3, 11 —

O God, hear us, hear our prayer.

Amen.

Entry of the Word

Old Testament Reading

Ruth 1:1–22

Prayer of Intercession

See page 40.

Response

New Testament reading

Galatians 3:28

Affirmation of Faith

It is the will of God
that no one should go away thirsty.

*It is the will of God
that all who ask will be received.*

It is the will of God
that none should be driven out of their homes
and communities.

*It is the will of God
that Christ's love be available to all the world.*

It is the will of God
that we should be a light
to a waiting and broken world.

*It is the will of God
that we love the world as Christ has loved us.*

Song

Lord's Prayer

Response

Reflection

We know that most of the uprooted people in this world are women and children. Forced from their homes to create new lives, they keep their families together and create new homes. Women are the nurturers of the family, and often the nurturers of their communities. In recognition that women too need nurturing and that children depend on adults for sustenance, while we sing the closing hymn, you are invited to come and pour some water on the plants in front of us. At the cross, at the tree of life, we find the one who makes us whole. At the cross, at the tree of life, the nations are healed. Go in the company of the one who treats us gently.

Thanks be to God.

In Chapljina, Bosnia with Grandmother Lucia

She sits in her half of a railroad car on a siding. This refugee "home" joins a long string of railroad cars; one provides cold water, others contain the community's toilets and kitchen. Her Bosnia village home was destroyed when armed troops deemed her lineage unacceptable. She sits with kerosene heaters and a gas stove providing scant heat and knits wool socks for her grandchildren and daughter living with her. Carrying water, washing clothes, passing time until the next meal from the common kitchen, the days stretch as endlessly as the tracks on which she sits. She prays for the safety of her other two daughters and five grandchildren lost in war's wasteland.

I rub her hands, cold and red from washing clothes and hanging them out on the fence. Her smile betrays her acceptance of comfort from a caring world. She resumes her task of using the donations of others to entrap love's warmth for her own. Her prayers to "Holy Papa" ask a better tomorrow for her family. She remembers happy years with her husband on the small farm, brutally taken by war. She remembers and waits with patience learned over 74 years. She and thousands of Bosnian Grandmothers sit on trains that go nowhere and wait.

Written after a 1995 visit to Bosnia by Paul Wilson, Church World Service Europe Office Director. Used with permission. Text from *For the Healing of the Nations*, Church World Service Office on Global Education (OGE), 2115 N. Charles Street, Baltimore, MD 21218-5755; phone: 410-727-6106; fax: 410-727-6108.

Indonesia. Boy who arrived from Vietnam on a boat attends school at Galang Island refugee camp.

UNHCR / 18198 / 04.1988 / J.–M. Micaud

Reflections
&
Poems

A Celtic Rune _

of Hospitality

I saw a stranger today
I put food for him in the eating-place
And drink in the drinking-place
And music in the listening-place.
In the Holy Name of the Trinity
He blessed myself and my house
My goods and my family.
And the lark said in her warble
Often, often, often
Goes Christ in the stranger's guise
Oh, oft and oft and oft,
Goes Christ in the Stranger's guise.

Reprinted from *Gloria Deo*, Worship Book for CEC Assembly IX, Stirling, Scotland, Conference of European Churches, Geneva: 1986, p. 118.

What is a Refugee?

What is a refugee?
Well and good to answer.
To answer such a question we need to be careful,
    because those who can answer it are very rare in this world.
To answer such a question, needs you first to take refuge,
    otherwise your answer will be simple and meaningless.
As refugees, we are victims of violence and war.
We left our motherland
    because we were being mistreated in many ways.
We ran to get protection in other countries.
But as a refugee, you are always simple in front of anybody.
You are subject to prejudice and mistaken always.
You can pass through any disaster
    and nobody will care about you.
Oh! What is lovely like our homeland?
In your own country, you are free,
    free like a butterfly when it flies from flower to flower,
    free like a fish moving in the water.
Homeland is a second heaven.
Without your home
    you are like a dog without a tail.
Give us peace,
    to return back to our beloved country,
      our precious heaven Sudan.
Give us our ancestors' land.
Africa, live in peace forever!

Andrew Mayak, The Sudan written in the Kakuma Refugee Camp, northwestern Kenya, 1995. From *TILTINGcages: An Anthology of Refugee Writings*, Naomi Flutter and Carl Solomon, ed., Pyrmont, Australia, 1995.

A City to Dwell In ___

Some wandered in desert wastes,
finding no way to a city to dwell in;
hungry and thirsty, their soul fainted within them.
Then they cried to the Lord in their trouble,
and he delivered them from their distress;
he led them by a straight way,
till they reached a city to dwell in.

— Psalm 107:4–7 RSV —

Ignacio spoke indignantly about the loss of his good jacket. When he was put in prison after his arrest, they had taken all his clothes and given him only a dirty T-shirt to wear with his shorts. A week later when they released him, someone had stolen his jacket, he had caught pneumonia and was threatened with the loss of one eye.

For Ignacio the theft of his jacket by prison authorities was the crowning indignity to a degrading process. Ignacio Lopez worked on behalf of Kaqchikel Presbytery with internal refugees, landless in Guatemala City. After a lengthy process of demonstration, petition and negotiation, the authorities had promised some vacant land for a housing project. Promises, promises, promises — but no action.

Again the people demonstrated; they asked to speak to the president of the bank who was supposed to make the land available. When the president did not show up, the demonstrators decided to wait him out. At this point police arrived to break up the demonstration which had been peaceful and orderly. Ignacio and other leaders were arrested in the resulting disturbance. The people have not yet received their land and now Ignacio has lost his jacket.

From *The Wounds of Manuel Saquic*, Jim Manley. Toronto: The United Church Publishing House, 1997.

In Guatemala, and throughout the world, people are moving from the country into the city. Wealth and bright lights suggest opportunity for everyone, even for poor people from the country. The reality of the city, power pyramids, pollution, and political indifference betrays this promise. Too often, recent arrivals can find neither jobs nor housing.

In Hebrew and Christian scriptures, Jerusalem is seen as more than one city among others; Jerusalem symbolizes all human cities where wealth is flaunted in the face of poverty, where power is maintained by violence.

The prophet Isaiah speaks to modern cities in today's world as well as to ancient Jerusalem:

> How the faithful city has become a whore!
> She that was full of justice,
> righteousness lodged in her— but now murderers!
> Your silver has become dross, your wine is mixed with water.
> Your princes are rebels and companions of thieves.
> Everyone loves a bribe and runs after gifts.
> They do not defend the orphan
> and the widow's cause does not come before them.
>
> — Isaiah 1:21–23 —

But if Jerusalem stands for human violence and oppression it also stands for humanity's highest hope, a human community where people live in co-operation with one another and in communion with God. The great poet who wrote the last part of Isaiah sees this new Jerusalem as more than a human creation; the new Jerusalem is the work of God.

> Be glad and rejoice forever in what I am creating;
> for behold I am about to create Jerusalem as a joy,
> and its people as a delight.
> I will rejoice in Jerusalem, and delight in my people;
> no more shall the sound of weeping be heard in it,
> or the cry of distress.
>
> — Isaiah 65:18–19 —

Does this mean that we are simply to wait with patient faith for God to accomplish this in its appointed time? Does not God work within us, calling us to help in building the city: the new Jerusalem? the new Vancouver? the new Calcutta, the new Guatemala? Is it not the Spirit of God working through people like Ignacio and the landless campesinos trying to build that human community?

Prayer

God, you call us into community with yourself and with one another; you want us to make our towns and cities places of justice and co-operation where everyone can flourish, everyone can create, everyone can find a place. We have so much to do before this happens in the place where we live. Help us, God, to build our city. In Jesus' name we pray. Amen.

Outport People

Outports are small fishing communities along the coastline of Newfoundland, Canada. Many people are no longer able to make a living fishing because the cod stocks have been depleted; they have been forced to leave the communities that have been home to their families for generations to search for work in other parts of Canada.

Don't take a man from the soil that he knows
Plant him elsewhere and expect him to grow.
And for God's Sake,
    don't tell him how much greener's the grass
For the uprooted people saw it wither too fast.

You can launch a house easy and tow it away
But the home doesn't move, it continues to stay
And the dollars you make sure it'll keep you alive
But they won't soothe the heart
And they can't ease the mind.

He spits on a plank and the memories roll.
The spring sun is shining, there's a lop in the cove
And the shoreline is dotted with lobster pot buoys
But his boat's full of weeds
    and there's tears in his eyes.

Don't take a man from the life that he knows
And tear up his roots and expect him to grow
Cause if he's unwillingly forced to decide
He'll move without leaving and never arrive.

Written by Bud Davidge, recorded by Simani, 1983. Used with permission.

____ You Have Come from Afar __

You have come from afar
    and waited long and are wearied:
Let us sit side by side
    sharing the same bread
    drawn from the same source
    to quiet the same hunger
    that makes us weak.
Then standing together
    let us share the same spirit,
    the same thoughts
    that once again draw us together
    in friendship and unity and peace.

Prières d'Ozawarnick, Canadian Indian liturgy. Excerpt from *World Hunger Resource: Gleanings of Spirit*, produced by the Church World Service Office on Global Education (OGE), Baltimore, MD.

Our "Home" is the realm of God.
It is where love and justice prevail,
    and we are called by God
    to make wherever we are
    as much like home as possible.
We dare not feel "at home" in a world like this;
    where one-third of the people live abundantly,
    and two-thirds live in scarcity –
Two ghettos: one rich, the other poor.
In such a world we are refugees
    dwelling on either side of a dividing wall
    afraid to cross the boundary.
Christ breaks down the dividing wall.
"Home" happens when the walls come down,
    and the ghettos are no more,
    and we are all brothers and sisters.
The beginning of the way home
    is the way of sharing!
Our footsteps down this aisle
    to share with others
    are the first short steps
    of the long journey "home."

Richard Wilcox, Spain. From *Gifts of Many Cultures: Worship Resources for the Global Community* © 1995 Maren C. Tirabassi and Kathy Wonson Eddy, United Church Press, Cleveland, Ohio, 44115.

The Story of Ruth __

In western societies, the story of Ruth is read at eight out of ten
Christian weddings. In a sloppy, sentimental way, she is depicted
as a romantic, rather submissive. The lyrical poetry of the "where
you go, I will go" is remembered as a love poem. It is a love poem,
but of a truly radical nature. Let us look closer.

> Naomi, Elimelech and their two sons were environmental
> refugees. Forced to migrate because of an enduring famine,
> they sought refuge in a neighbouring country that appears
> to have been welcoming to these strangers. In Moab, the
> sons married Moabite women: Ruth and Orpah. Time
> passed. Naomi's sons and husband died, leaving the women
> in a precarious situation. Without male kin, these women
> had no status nor right to property. Given the traditions of
> the time, Ruth and Orpah could have returned to their fa-
> ther's home and sought re-marriage from within their own
> community. Naomi, though, had no option but to return to
> Bethlehem and petition the support of whatever kin she
> could locate. Her situation was not unlike many migrant
> women of today.
>
> For reasons which remain unclear from the text, Ruth
> opts to follow Naomi. Despite forceful objections from the
> mother-in-law, she passionately states "where you go, I will
> go. Your God will be my God." Courageous determined,
> resourceful, devoted.
>
> It is not a timid, submissive person who makes this radi-
> cal choice to risk a perilous journey, leading to an uncertain

Excerpts from a homily by the Rev. Glynnis Williams at the consultation The Prophetic
Mission of Churches in Response to Forced Displacement of People held in Addis Ababa,
Ethiopia, November 1995, co-sponsored by Caritas Internationalis, Lutheran World Fed-
eration/World Service, and the World Council of Churches.

future. The legacy of Ruth is one of courage and faith. The story of Ruth is written in a particular context. The people of Israel had been scattered in exile, plagued by famine and other disasters. As they returned to the homeland, there was an understandable desire to make sense of these events in the terms they knew best: religious terms.

They had questions such as: Where was God? Why had God abandoned the chosen people? Why was God punishing them? They needed to make sense of the tragedy.

In Ruth's social context, one explanation was provided by Ezra and Nehemiah. These voices of religious authority preached that the catastrophes were the consequence of the sin of contamination by pagans. Specifically they blamed the sin of the Israelite men who had married foreign women while in exile. Their solution: the ancient equivalent of ethnic cleansing. Ezra chapter 10 says "make confession to the Lord, the God of your ancestors, and do his will: separate yourselves from your foreign wives." Foreign women were blamed for the sin of Solomon, the great Israelite king. As a consequence, hundreds of thousands of wives and children were violently expelled from the country, disowned by their husbands and fathers to wander and fend for themselves. Marriage to foreign women was an abomination.

On one side of the street, from the pulpit of the synagogue was the priest preaching the guild of the foreigner. It was the foreigner who had led the Israelites astray and brought on the wrath of God.

Down the street on the other side was another priest, perhaps the writer of the book of Ruth, lifting up her courage and faithfulness. For this person, Ruth was the virtuous one. In direct opposition to the voices of fear and superstition, Ruth was held up as the woman who brought redemption, not sin.

In my country [Canada] there are voices which proclaim that we have too many refugees and immigrants; that it is the foreigners who are responsible for the economic hard times and unemployment that has increased in recent years.

My friends, as the philosopher Ecclesiastes says, "there

is nothing new under the sun," the voices of xenophobia are both ancient and contemporary. And the community of believers is not exempt from this interpretation.

The returning migrants to Judah were confronted with two traditions within the same religion. Their need to make sense of their history, their suffering and the temptation to scapegoat the foreigner was overwhelming, but other voices offered another wisdom. The uprooted woman, Ruth, became the symbol of resistance to this spiteful hatred.

Sisters and brothers, you and I are called, indeed compelled, to stand in the tradition of Ruth. To state that it is not the migrant, the refugee, who is the cause of economic problems or crime. To state that hatred and racism are not the ways of God.

The prophet Ruth challenges each one of us, whether we have lived the experience of forced displacement or are advocates standing with those who have been displaced.

Find the strength of Ruth to respond with passion and compassion. God has promised to be with us as we respond in the tradition of Ruth to the forces in our world that work against the love and justice of Jesus Christ.

Tanzania.
Refugees from
Rwanda at
Benaco Camp use
supplied firewood.

UNHCR / C. Sattlberger

A Psalm for the Displaced

God, our promised land;
Christ, our way,
    our journey has become long and hard
    because we wander about like nomads
    not knowing where to go.
We are strangers in our own land,
    without bread, a roof, a future.
But you came to find us
    with your life-giving breath.
You, who are also displaced,
    have become an exile with us.
You offer us anew the promised land.
Your spirit urges us toward
    that joyous homecoming.

Displaced campesinos, Lima, Peru, *Psalms for Life and Peace*, Latinamerica Press, November 5, 1987

A Christmas Message

Jesus was born away from home while his parents were on the move against their will, forced to go to Bethlehem for a census. The gospel of Matthew tells us that soon after his birth the family had to flee to Egypt to escape persecution.

Today, to remember and celebrate the birth of Jesus Christ is to do so in a world where millions of people are also compelled to be on the move: refugees driven from their towns and villages by war, children on the road without a home, asylum seekers rejected and deported from a country of refuge, migrants separated from their families. They all knock at our door. Will we open it for them?

In Jesus Christ, God came into our human world. But God came as a stranger, unacknowledged. There was no place for the one sent by God, and finally he was pushed out of the world and on to a cross as a criminal. This Christmas, God is still on the move with the millions of uprooted people who look for a safe place to be received...

In the encounter with the stranger we encounter God. In Jesus Christ, God has come into our midst. But God remains an unwanted alien. God shares the lot of those who do not fit our acceptable categories. To this day, people try to prove that Jesus' claim to have been sent by God was illegitimate, just as many western governments seek to prove refugees and asylum seekers are bogus.

For those who do receive God in Christ, the world changes. To encounter God is to encounter truth and to discover that we are children of God. God is still on the move to us. We can close the door to God. We do so every time we deny an uprooted person safety and sanctuary. We can also open the door. In the refugee, the migrant, the internally displaced, Jesus comes to us again this Christmas. To allow him entry is to receive God — the stranger who wants to share our lives!

Dr. Konrad Raiser, General Secretary of the World Council of Churches, 1997.

Our Land is the Ixcán

During 1978–1984, forced disappearances, rape, torture and assassinations were commonplace in Guatemala. The military's counter-insurgency forces massacred hundreds of Mayan peasants and burned to the ground some 440 villages. The Mayans fled into the mountains, where they lived in campsites under the cover of thick bush and trees to avoid being detected by helicopter patrols. Beginning in 1992, these Communities of Populations in Resistance or CPRs as they are known, were able to leave the mountains to establish settlements in the open. To mark their re-emergence, the CPRs in the Ixcán region published an audio-cassette of their songs. These are the lyrics to one of them.

Our land is the Ixcán,
lovely and mountainous.
There is also the thick undergrowth
And all is encircled by hillocks.

> We are located in the midst
> of our great rivers
> the Ixcán and the Xalbal
> And the unyielding Cuache hills.

Hundreds of soldiers came to hunt for us
crossing the mountains and the thickets
intending to come and put an end to us
so they could take over our lands.

> *They have used planes and helicopters,*
> *machine gunning and bombing us,*
> *but they haven't been able to finish us off*
> *and they never will.*

From an audio-cassette of eleven songs of the CPRs recorded in Ixcán.

Thanks to our mountains
that give us protection
the land is ours and
we are able to work on it.

> And so, as compañeros
> always thinking of our God
> we will continue to work
> defending our lands.

Hundreds of soldiers came to hunt for us
crossing the mountains and the thickets
intending to come and put an end to us
so they could take over our lands.

> *They have used planes and helicopters,*
> *machine gunning and bombing us,*
> *but they haven't been able to finish us off*
> *and they never will.*

> We are a civilian population.
> We want peace and tranquillity.
> Enough of repression!
> Let there be a better life.

We demand that the government
 pull out its armed forces
in the area of Ixcán;
that they stop persecuting us.

> We bid farewell to our compañeros
> listening to us in other places.
> Now there are thousands of us resisting,
> struggling in the mountains
> > these 12 years.

Declaration of the __
Penan People, Borneo

The forest is our livelihood. We have lived here before any of you outsiders came. We fished in clean rivers and hunted in the jungle. We made our sago meat and ate fruit of trees. Our life was not easy but we lived it in content. Now the logging companies turn rivers into muddy streams and the jungle into devastation. The fish cannot survive in dirty rivers and wild animals will not live in devastated forests. You took advantage of our trusting nature and cheated us into unfair deals. By your doing, you have taken away our livelihood and threaten our very lives. We want our ancestral land, the land we live on, back. We can use it in a wiser way. When you come to us, come as guests, with respect.

From *Dare to Dream*, compiled and edited by Geoffrey Duncan. Fount: London, 1995.

Kenya. Refugees from Somalia, Dadaab Camp, participate in tree-planting to reforest damaged land, retain water in the soil and resist erosion.

UNHCR / 26032 / 05.1996 / W. Stone

The Heart of God

The heart of God is one with the stranger.

In Deuteronomy 26:5 the Hebrew people understand themselves as a wandering people. They are a people without a home; mistreated slaves in a strange land; uprooted people seeking shelter. Through all the misery, toil and oppression, they survive. They grow in numbers and finally build up their own community. Behind all this, the Hebrew people richly experience that there is a Heart caring for them, guiding them, never forsaking them. That is the Heart of God.

It is a Heart that takes their side. God is always on their side. No matter how weak they are, how wrong they are, how miserable they are, how stubborn they are, God is always with them. God is just, yet not judgemental. God is holy, yet not detached. Like a faithful companion, God is journeying with them. That is the Heart of God.

From "Becoming a Church of the Stranger," a Bible study produced by the Christian Conference of Asia, June, 1997.

Migrant

Stranger in your homeland and stranger
amongst strangers
month after month you labour and every day
is the same as yesterday.
But for you also there comes
the happiest of days
That in which you return home:
and once you are home
the misunderstandings begin.
Your children have grown
of you all they know is your name
but your affection, your love is enough
to draw them all
to your heart
and the old tie is remade.
Your dreamed-of days
have vanished quickly
you go — and the old round begins.
Your soul once again you leave here
and alone, with your bag
filled with memories you go:
This is your whole life consumed
between an arrival and a departure
and to think that you went
to stay for only a year or two.

Rosa Coppola. From *Balai*, Asian Journal No. 12, as printed in *A Moment to Choose: Risking to be with Uprooted Peoples*, A Resource Book produced by the World Council of Churches, 1996.

Isaiah's Song of Hope

A poem for all ages

This poem was written for children, and also could be used with a group of people of all ages.

Isaiah the prophet lived a long time ago in the city of Jerusalem. Most people in his country were very scared. There had been a terrible war. What used to be one country had become two countries. The North and the South ended up fighting and the whole country split in half to become the Northern and Southern Kingdoms. Lots of people were killed and many parts of Jerusalem were destroyed.

Then there was an even bigger problem. The huge empire of Assyria had taken over the whole of the Northern Kingdom. Lots of people were taken far from their home. Many people were afraid Jerusalem would be next.

In the middle of this terrible time, people became more and more frightened. They began to feel hopeless. Isaiah wrote poems. He wrote a beautiful poem to remind people that God would care for them even in hard times, and that some day there would be no more fighting and no more refugees.

A suggestion for presenting the poem in a group: Read Isaiah's Poem *slowly. You may wish to divide up verses of the poem and create a percussion accompaniment to the verses. Depending on group size you might work as a whole group or divide into small groups. Don't make the accompaniment so loud that it blocks out the words. Try to say the words together in rhythm and let the instruments add to the mood or feeling. For example, the first verse might have a fearful shaking feeling, the second verse*

Based on Isaiah 2:1–4. Alyson Huntly, Canada. From *The Whole People of God Curriculum* © 1995 Wood Lake Books Inc. Used with permission.

might be like soft walking and listening, the fourth verse might be loud as the swords are beaten into plows, the final verse might be strong and joyful, etc.

Isaiah's Poem

Do not cower, do not hide,
Do not run away in fear.
In the days that are to come
God will always be right here.
For God's holy place will be
Like the tallest mountain peak
And all people of the earth
Will come near to hear God speak.
They will learn to walk God's ways
They will learn to do what's right
They will let God be the one
To help settle all their fights.
They will break their swords and spears
They will bend and beat
Them into plows to till their fields
And grow food for all to eat.
No one will be taught to fight
Wars and battles all will end
In the days that are to come
All the nations will be friends.

Who Are They?

Uprooted people are struggling to be actors and shapers of their lives. They are not faceless numbers out there. They are our brothers and sisters. We worship, work, live, struggle, cry, laugh, celebrate with them. We [need to] take time to close our eyes and open our hearts to again see their faces, to feel their suffering, their struggle and, most of all, their courage, determination and dignity.

From a communiqué issued at a meeting of the World Council of Churches Global Ecumenical Network for Uprooted People, March 1997.

Joseph's Story

The immediacy of the holy family's departure into exile is striking. The need for immediate flight from danger is a typical situation for the majority of refugees. As the Church in The Gambia, we are confronted daily with the pain of refugees who have fled from conflict.

Let me share with you the story of another Joseph, from Sierra Leone. He was working with his two small children in the family garden several hundred metres away when rebels hit the village. The children hid. Joseph ran to search for his wife and his other children. He found the house on fire, terror and chaos in the village, but no sign of his family. He came straight to The Gambia with the two children, but has since returned in search of his wife whom he has heard was alive but injured. As with the biblical Joseph, he has placed the lives of himself and his family in God's hands, seeing Him as his only hope.

From a homily by Rt. Rev. S. Tilewa Johnson, Bishop of Gambia

Lord, No One

Is a Stranger to You

Lord, no one is a stranger to you
and no one is ever far from
your loving care.
In your kindness watch over refugees
and exiles,
those separated from their loved ones,
young people who are lost,
and those who have left or run away
from home.
Bring them back safely to the place
where they long to be
and help us always to show your kindness
to strangers and to those in need.

From "Stay With Us: Worship Resources," CAFOD, London, England.

By the rivers of foreign countries we sat down as refugees;
there we wept when we remembered the land of our birth.
We stopped singing our beloved songs of liberation.
Those who are helping our enemies wanted us to sing;
they wanted us to entertain them:
Sing us a song about the land whence you fled.

How can they expect us to entertain them
with our suffering and tears?
May I never turn our struggle for freedom and peace
into entertainments for those who are friends of our enemies!
May I never be able to sing again
if I do not remember you,
if I do not think of you,
O country of my birth!

Remember, Lord, what the oppressors did
the day they turned us into refugees.
Remember how they kept saying,
Let us destroy them completely!

From Namibia. World Council of Churches Publications, 1986.

Strangers before God

In Jesus the Christ who was made a stranger by his own people, God has reached out to those far off and identified with them. Before God, we are all strangers who lack status and recognition, but through Christ we are no longer aliens and strangers, but citizens of God's commonwealth and members of God's household.

Our new identity as children of God is given to us without merit, as a pure gift of God's grace. We will keep this identity only as long as we share it with others, especially with those who have lost the right to a recognized identity, for in them we encounter Christ the stranger. He meets us in unexpected places and under the most unlikely disguises, seeking recognition and response. We shall know only when we are fully known, when we shall see him in full clarity.

This is the message of the parable of the Last Judgement which allows us to take a look at who we truly are from the perspective of God. Therefore, it is an urgent invitation to the churches to rediscover their identity as church of the stranger. May God open our eyes, that we may see, and give us courage to do what is right.

Rev. Dr. Konrad Raiser, General Secretary, World Council of Churches From a sermon on the occasion of the launch of the Ecumenical Year of Churches in Solidarity with Uprooted People, Geneva, Switzerland, March 4, 1997.

The Kite As Our Hope

The kite is the symbol for our hope and faith!
The kite flies freely even as its string is held securely
    in someone's hand.
Our hope rises and soars
    above the cruel reality of our lives —
    even as our faith is secure in God who
    accompanies us in our struggle.
Yes! Even now God is using our efforts
    to bring a new day when all people
    will be free from oppression –
    when we shall be free to provide for
    the basic needs of our loved ones.
The kite flies freely as our hope soars

IN DEFENSE OF LIFE!

Written by the Colombian delegation to the Sao Paulo Process Regional Meeting in Lima, Peru, 1994, a gathering of church workers from North America, Latin America, and the Caribbean convened by Church World Service. From *For the Healing of the Nations*, Office on Global Education, Baltimore, MD, USA.

Receiving the Stranger

We must genuinely receive the stranger. In theological terms, we must incorporate their lives into ours so that we can know the unity which we share as children of God. What these encounters invariably teach us is the common humanity which we share. Once ethnic, racial, and cultural differences are peeled away, the possibility of experiencing our common humanity emerges. Therefore, tolerating the stranger is not enough. Accepting the stranger as a sister or brother is what is required. Only then are we blessed. Only then is their spirit and ours united.

C. Richard Parkins, director, Episcopal Migration Ministries, USA.

Guatemala. Refugees who have voluntary returned from Mexico arrive at Cobán.

UNHCR / 18196 / 02.1988 / D. Bregnard

Tinsel sways like ghosts
    in the half light and bitter
    wind of opening door,
    candles flicker, too.
Another stranger has come
    seeking money
    in the cold Advent night.
Hard times drive many here
    to the parsonage door.
Some, ashamed to beg, first time,
    but hungry and too poor
    for Christmas, please,
    my children are crying,
    please, lady.
Others have grown smooth,
    rehearsed pleas, tough
    against denial, damning
    gratitude, never enough,
    angry at me
    for my home,
    more, lady.
Others, weak or drunk,
    exhausted by want,
    mumble words, words,
    it doesn't matter, look at my face,
    knowing I'll give
    or not —

Maren C. Tirabassi, U.S.A. From *Gifts of Many Cultures: Worship Resources for the Global Community* © 1995 Maren C. Tirabassi and Kathy Wonson Eddy, United Church Press, Cleveland, Ohio, 44115.

give so I can
shut the door
on the cold,
    give, lady.
The bell rings again.
Another stranger has come
    in the cold Advent night —
I search the face
    for Christ.
Yes, yes —
        there he is,
            there he is,
                there he is.

Refugees and Strangers
A Drama

You may choose different players for each character. The Protest could be made by different voices from a large, self-confident group on centre stage. You could intersperse the drama with silence, music or prayer to change the atmosphere from time to time

Speaker: My name is Abraham. We have just come to this place called Canaan. It's not our home, but God has called us to live here. We've brought our belongings, but we haven't got many relatives with us who could look after us if we get sick. We're rather old you see.

Protest: Stop! Of course you can't stay here! There's no place here for anyone who can't look after himself. We've never heard of anything so ridiculous! God called you indeed! Where would we be if all the old people who can no longer work came to us? We didn't ask you to come! Go home and sort yourselves out!

Speaker: My name is Jacob.
I'm running away because I've got myself into trouble at home. I couldn't possibly go back; my brother would kill me. Now I'm in this strange place. I'd like to stay here and get a job, but it's hard to know if you can trust new people. What will they think of me? Will they treat me fairly, or will they try to cheat me?

Adapted from a piece by Renate Becher for the European Methodist Youth Council Network.

Protest: Move on somewhere else you good-for-nothing! We're decent people here and we don't want anything to do with the likes of you! You'll cause just as much trouble here, and none of us will feel safe any more.

Speaker: My name is Joseph. My brothers have sold me as a slave to a man called Potiphar. They were jealous of me — and I have to be honest, I didn't always behave well towards them. That Potiphar's wife tells nasty stories about me. Will he believe me or her? I am a stranger here, and I worry that people will blame me for every bad thing that happens. Will I have any rights in this land?

Protest: What? You can't expect us to believe a word you say if even your own brothers wanted to get rid of you! We've met your kind before, and we've got far too many foreigners here already. We're going to watch every single thing you do, because you can't be trusted and then we'll think about what to do with you.

Speaker: My name is Moses. I was standing up for one of my own people when I hit an Egyptian who was bullying us. The Egyptians think that if we hit one of them, that is as bad as committing a murder. So now I've had to go into hiding. What is going to happen to me? I'm terrified that they will catch me and kill me.

Protest: You hit an Egyptian?! Well that's the last straw! There's no place for a thug like you in a civilised country like this. We're going to send you back to your own country!

Speaker: My name is Ruth. I came here to Bethlehem with my mother-in-law, Naomi. We are widows. We have no children, and no money. Naomi is too old to work any more. Will anyone give me a job, so that I can earn enough to feed us both? We don't want any charity. We could never take something for nothing.

Protest: For goodness sake! Enough is enough! Are we the poorhouse of the world? Haven't we got enough poor people of our own?! No, you can't stay here sponging off us!

Speaker: My name is Daniel. I'm living here in the King's palace. We're a bit worried because my friends and I have a different religion, and we live in a different way from the people around us. Will they accept that?

Protest: Of course we won't! You're foreigners aren't you! If you want to live here, you'll have to behave like the rest of u. Why does your sort always have to be different?

Speaker: My name is Mary. I've come to Bethlehem with my husband, Joseph. I'm having a baby and we're desperate to find me where to stay for a while. My baby could be born at any time now, and I need a warm room and a bed. We're very poor. Will anyone take us in?

Protest: Now listen here once and for all. If you want anything in this world, you've got to pay for it! Haven't you got any shame? Bringing children into this world when you have no money to look after them! And then to expect handouts!

Speaker: My name is Joseph. I've had to flee as fast as possible with my wife Mary and our baby, Jesus. King Herod wanted to kill him. Now we've almost reached Egypt. Will the Egyptians let us into their country? What will happen to us if they send us back to Nazareth?

Protest: Who knows and who cares? This family could be more trouble than they're worth. They could make life difficult for all of us.

Call No One Stranger

This poem can be read by many different voices or by one.

You first saw them by the roadside
    standing at the crossroads, waiting...
    listening...watching
They walked in silence, small bundles on their backs
    clutching other bits in their hands.
Fear on the faces of those women, men and children.
Frightened by the past, fearful of the future
Will no one understand their pain?
Will anyone open a door to receive them?
Look again and you will see
    familiar people...
    mothers and fathers,
    sisters and brothers,
    grandparents.
Listen and you will hear
    familiar sounds...
    talking, crying, laughing.
Understand and you will know
    the stuff of which your dreams are made...
    love and laughter, security and safety,
    peace and prosperity...
    are their dreams too.
That which is joy to every human heart
    is not alien to theirs
The peace you long for is that same peace
    they strive for.

Sr. Patricia Mulhall. From "Who is My Neighbour?" CAFOD, London, England.

We stand together as one…
    drawing warmth from the same sun and
    life from the same earth
And though we travel on different roads
We're part of one God, one Earth, one Universe…
There are no strangers.
Tears shed in compassion…
    songs of love and dreams of peace
    make us all one.
Recognise your family in the stranger
Open your door, invite them in
    to sit at your table
    and share your bread.
Call no one stranger
    whose roots are kin to your own…
    whose lives all spring from the
One Great Fountain of Life!